The Wild West in American History

CATTLE RANCHERS

Written by Harriet Upton
Illustrated by James Rownd
Edited by Arlene C. Rourke

© 1990 by Rourke Publications, Inc.

Library of Congress Cataloging-in-Publication Data

Upton, Harriet, 1945-
  Cattle ranchers.
    p. cm. —(The Wild West in American history)
  Summary: Discusses the significance of the early cattle ranchers to the development of the Wild West..
    1. Ranch life—West (U.S.)—History—19th century—Juvenile literature. 2. Ranchers—West (U.S.)—History—19th century—Juvenile literature. 3. Frontier and pioneer life—West (U.S.)—Juvenile literature. 4. Cattle trade—West (U.S.)—History—19th century—Juvenile literature. 5. West (U.S.)—History—1848-1950—Juvenile literature. [1. Ranch life—West (U.S.)—History—19th century. 2. Ranchers—West (U.S.)—History—19th century. 3. Frontier and pioneer life—West (U.S.) 4. West (U.S.)—History—1848-1950.] I. Title. II. Series.
F596.U68 1990
978   89-24259
                                  CIP
  ISBN 0-86625-372-6   AC

Rourke Publications, Inc.
Vero Beach, Florida 32964

CATTLE RANCHERS

SCENE NEAR ALICE TEXAS   M 209

(Photo courtesy of Texas Historical Society.)

CATTLE RANCHERS

While the cowboy has always captured the imagination of the public, it is the rancher who made the greater contribution to American history. Many early ranchers were, of course, former cowboys or trail drivers themselves.

The West's first ranches were established almost one hundred and fifty years ago. By the 1880s, many large ranching operations dotted the vast stretches of land from Texas to Montana and Kansas to California. The first ranchers set out to conquer their environment, to build something where nothing had previously existed. As early settlers and businessmen, they shaped the culture and the politics of the West.

The successful rancher held a variety of roles. He worked alongside his hired hands one day and rubbed elbows with senators and governors the next. He was a family man, a community man, and a businessman. A rancher's hospitality was famous— no matter who stopped in, he was welcomed with a good meal and a bed for the night. It was all part of the cattleman's code of ethics, a code that sometimes also included taking the law into his own hands.

EARLY RANCHERS

*N*ot long after Texas joined the Union in 1845, word went out that the new state was the perfect place for ranching. Texas had good grazing lands and mild winters. According to optimistic reports, anyone who took up ranching in Texas was sure to become wealthy!

Cattle were already being raised in many states east of the Mississippi. In areas where it was easy to grow corn and other feed for stock, cattle were plentiful and were kept confined to certain pastures. In other areas, such as Kentucky, Tennessee, and North Carolina, cattle were branded and allowed to roam in the woods and fields in search of food. At market time they were rounded up to be sold.

For the most part, the ranching industry of the West had less in common with the cattle farms in the eastern U.S. and more in common with Mexican *ranchos*. The Mexican system was itself a product of the Spanish *conquistadores*. The ranch was set up with a corral, and the horsegear, such as the style of bit and saddle, came from the Spanish. So did the rider's clothing, including the broad-brimmed hat, spurs, and leather *chaperajos*. Of course, without the Spanish, there might have been no ranching industry at all—it was the Spanish who first brought cattle to the New World.

The clothing worn by the Mexican cowboy inspired cowboys in the western United States.

During the 1840s and 1850s, as pioneers began emigrating west on the Oregon Trail, enterprising cattlemen took advantage of the opportunity to make money. These men maintained small herds at points along the trail and exchanged fresh steers for trail-weary, skinny oxen at a nice profit. There was nothing wrong with the cattle they acquired that a few months of good grazing wouldn't cure. Some traders also supplied feed for the emigrants' cattle and sold cattle to miners, military personnel, and other people who were working in the West.

These early ranchers seldom had much knowledge of cattle before they became cattlemen. Some had come west with the Gold Rush of 1849. When they didn't make their fortunes in gold, they turned to trading cattle instead. Others, the sons of early pioneer farmers, saw opportunity knocking at their back doors. Later, more would arrive because of the climate, which was good for those with fragile constitutions, or solely because they had plenty of money and saw ranching as an easy and profitable investment.

THE KING RANCH

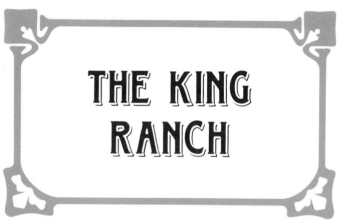

Richard King was born in New York City in 1825. His parents were Irish immigrants, and his family was poor. At the age of eleven, he left home and wound up as a stowaway on a ship headed for the Gulf of Mexico. When discovered, he convinced the captain to let him work as a cabin boy. Arriving in Louisiana, he found work on boats and studied to become a ship's captain. In 1846, during the Mexican War, he ferried supplies on the Rio Grande in Texas. After the war, he and a friend, Mifflin Kenedy, bought government surplus riverboats and started a riverboat company that brought them a respectable income.

King, however, was restless and ambitious, and before long he was looking for more ways to make money. On an 1852 trip to Corpus Christi from Brownsville, Texas, he saw the land on which he would put his ranch. Strong trees and sweet prairie grasses grew there, and through it ran a stream called the Santa Gertrudis. King knew that there were problems still to be solved in the cattle industry. There were people back East willing to pay up to thirty dollars a head for cattle, but there was no way to deliver the cattle to them. King decided to take the risk anyway and invested his modest savings in the cattle ranch.

From then on, whenever King wasn't working at the riverboat company, he was at the ranch. He dammed up a stream to create a reservoir, which would assure a ready supply of water. He erected a cabin and outbuildings and began buying animals. To tend the animals, he hired Mexican *vaqueros*—in fact, he hired a whole village! Over one hundred Mexicans moved to the Santa Gertrudis and built homes on King's property. He became their patrón, and they became *Los Kineños*, or King people. Everyone

on the ranch had a job, creating a self-sufficient community similar to a small town.

A hard worker himself, King demanded a lot from his hired hands but, at the same time, was extremely fair with them. For that he was respected and liked. He was also a visionary, looking to the future and anticipating its opportunities. One of King's most brilliant moves was to import Eastern beef cattle for breeding with his Texas longhorns. The longhorn was a hardy animal, a survivor that needed little water to exist in semi-desert conditions. The Texas longhorns were descendants of Mexican cattle that had been abandoned and left to fend for themselves. They were sold mainly for their hides and for their fat, which was used to make soap and candles. The Eastern breeds, while not nearly as rugged, produced considerably more meat, and the meat was more tender. King's controlled experiments produced a crossbreed that combined the best of the longhorn and the Durham. He named his new breed Santa Gertrudis.

There was always work for ranch hands.

Richard King.
(Photo courtesy of Texas Historical Society.)

In 1861 the Civil War began, disrupting King's ranching operations and throwing smaller and less stable ranches into ruin. Texas was fighting on the side of the South, and most ranch hands left to become soldiers. King, too, supported the Confederacy, and he put his riverboat operation to work ferrying supplies and arms to the fighting men. The lost income from his ranching operations paled in comparison with the money he made on the river.

After the war, King's fortunes increased steadily. He continued to acquire land and enlarge his herds. By 1875, he was driving 60,000 head of cattle to market each year. At the same time, he was losing a significant number of cattle to rustlers, who could sell the cattle in Mexico for up to four dollars a head. Smaller ranch owners had already conceded to the rustlers, giving up their ranches, but King held out. In 1875, the ranch was attacked twice and a village near Corpus Christi was ravaged, setting off a riot between Mexicans and Texans. Finally, the government reorganized the Texas Rangers, who soon put a stop to the raids.

By the time King died in 1885, his ranch extended over 600,000 acres! It was so profitable that he had invested in other businesses as well. He was part owner of a city newspaper, a stagecoach line, an ice-making plant, and a railroad company.

RAILROADS TO THE RESCUE

The Civil War ended in 1865, with the North defeating the South. On the Texas plains, unattended cattle had been multiplying with no one to ride herd on them. Anyone who wanted could round them up and begin a ranching operation. Quite a few determined, energetic young men did just that. They needed to buy or homestead only a small section of land as headquarters because their herd could graze on public land at no cost.

In 1866, Texan ranchers ran into an obstacle in their attempts to drive these cattle to market. Farmers and ranchers along the trail were claiming that the Texas longhorns were carriers of a disease they called Spanish or Texas fever. The disease was spread by ticks that the cattle carried, and although the longhorns themselves were immune to the disease, herds of cattle along the way had been infected. No longer could the drovers take their cattle through eastern Kansas and southwestern Missouri.

Within a year, a solution to the problem emerged. In 1862, President Lincoln signed the Pacific Railroad Act, setting in motion the building of a transcontinental railroad that would stretch between Omaha, Nebraska, and Sacramento, California. Union Pacific was awarded the contract to build from the east going west.

By 1867, the Union Pacific Railway reached from Omaha southwest into the middle of Kansas. Along its way were the towns of Detroit, Abilene, and Solomon City. Joseph G. McCoy, a livestock trader, had the idea of setting up a stockyard at one of the towns on the rail line and shipping the cattle by train the rest of the way. Abilene, although technically within the quarantine area, was finally chosen. At first many townspeople resisted the idea, fearing for the welfare of the local livestock. As soon as they realized the great amounts of money that would be accompanying the cattle into Abilene,

Cattle ranching was a team effort. Here a group of cowboys lasso and brand the new calves.
(Photo courtesy of Wyoming State Archives.)

however, their resistance quickly melted away.

Joseph G. McCoy had grown up on a farm in Illinois and had followed his two brothers into the livestock trading business. William K. McCoy and Brothers was a profitable company. William stayed in New York City to look after the sales, James remained on the farm in Illinois to fatten up the cattle, and Joseph worked as Kansas manager, negotiating to buy Texas livestock.

By the time McCoy's plan was put into effect, the 1867 trail driving season was already in progress. The first year was slow. Only 35,000 head of cattle came to Abilene, and of those, between 18,000 and 20,000 were shipped to the East. One year later, over 52,000 head of cattle made the Union Pacific trip east from Abilene.

MONTANA'S FIRST CATTLEMEN

Among Montana's earliest ranchers were some of the same cattlemen who served the emigrants along the Oregon Trail. John Owen had come west as a storekeeper in the military. The regiment was bound for Oregon, but an early and threatening winter forced them to stop at Fort Hall in Idaho until spring. By then, Owen had decided to leave the military and remain where he was, certain he could make a good living trading with the emigrants.

That fall, in 1850, he went north into Montana Territory, admitted to the Union as a state in 1889. It happened that the priests who had begun St. Mary's Mission in 1841 had made plans to move farther west, and Owen was able to buy the mission and concentrate on building a herd of cattle.

Captain Richard Grant and his sons spent the same summer trading on the Mormon Trail between Fort Bridger and Salt Lake. They already lived in Montana—Grant was a former fur trapper and a retired Hudson's Bay supervisor who had settled with his wife in Jefferson Valley, not far from Owen. Mrs. Grant was part Indian, and their grown sons lived in tipis (tepees) near Grant's cabin with their own wives. The Grants' summer of trading had resulted in their initial herd of cattle, primarily European breeds that came from farms in the Middle West.

During the 1850s, the cattle industry in Montana grew. Cattle were ranged in the valleys of western Montana and then taken to markets in Utah, Idaho, and Oregon. It was through one of these markets in Utah that James and Granville Stuart and their friend, Reese Anderson, found their way to Montana. En route back to Iowa from California, they had been marooned at Malad Creek, Utah, in 1857. The locals and the U.S. Army were fighting, and all routes east and west were blocked. In the end, they went north to the Grants' ranch with their Malad Creek host, a cattle trader.

The Stuarts liked what they found and, instead of returning to Iowa, they became road traders. With the cattle they brought back, they were able to start their own spread at the mouth of Benetsee Creek, where gold had been discovered several years before. Their place, which became known as American Fork, proved to be a good resting stop for all kinds of travelers, from Oregon-bound emigrants, to gold seekers, to wandering mountain men. The Stuarts' Benetsee Creek never lived up to its promise of gold, but nearby locations did. That part of Montana soon became inundated with goldseekers.

The Stuart brothers prospered modestly during this gold rush—not by finding gold, but by selling goods to the miners. In 1862, they

A well-to-do ranching family enjoys a relaxing evening. (Photo courtesy of Oregon Historical Society.)

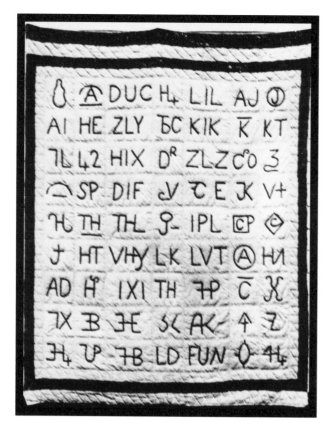

Art took many forms in the West. Mrs. Charles Eckhart sewed the Brand Quilt, showing early Bandera County brands.

(Photo courtesy of Texas Historical Society.)

moved to Bannack, well over one hundred miles south of Benetsee (now called Gold Creek). There they opened a butcher shop and sold their beef. They also became part owners of stores in Virginia City and Deer Lodge.

James Stuart died at the age of forty-two, while Granville Stuart lived to be eighty-four. During that time, he pursued many different occupations, none of which made him a millionaire. Though not formally educated, Granville was a voracious reader and a self-taught artist. Many of his sketches exist today, and they provide an authentic view of Montana during his time. He also wrote a book, *Montana As It Is*, which was published in New York in 1865. He was instrumental in founding the Historical Society of Montana.

In the 1870s, Granville Stuart went back into ranching, this time with Conrad Kohrs as a partner. Luck was not with him. The winter of 1886-1887 took its toll on their ranching operation. Kohrs stuck it out, but Stuart left the business. He never succeeded in becoming a rich man in his adopted state, but he did become a well known and highly respected one.

CONRAD KOHRS

*L*ike the Stuart brothers, Conrad Kohrs seized the opportunity to make money from the gold seekers that came to Montana. In 1862, at the age of twenty-six, he arrived in Deer Lodge Valley en route to the gold fields of Idaho. Originally from Europe, he had, according to one historian, "a kaleidoscopic career as cabin boy, grocery clerk, river raftsman, sausage salesman, California and Fraser River gold miner, with some experience as butcher and assistant in a brother-in-law's packing plant back in Davenport, Iowa."

Even will all these talents, Kohrs ran out of money. He wisely took a job butchering cows in Bannack for twenty-five dollars a month. His boss, involved in a local feud, left town shortly thereafter, and Kohrs inherited the business. When the miners left Bannack for Alder Gulch, so did Kohrs. There he went into partnership with Ben Peel, and they billed themselves as Con & Peel.

Kohrs' job was to acquire the cattle, while Peel minded the store. They were not wasteful; they used every part of the animal. They made sausage out of the parts of the cow that they didn't sell as steaks, and candles out of the tallow. As a place to keep their growing herd of cattle, they bought a ranch in the Deer Lodge Valley in 1865. Here Con & Peel worked at breeding their cattle with even better beef cattle. Peel decided not to stick it out. He left Montana to return to Missouri, and Kohrs bought him out. Kohrs also bought the Johnny Grant Ranch when Grant returned to Canada.

By the late 1870s, Kohrs had turned into a well-to-do rancher. When the opportunity arose, he bought into another large ranching operation and became partners with Granville Stuart. The DHS Ranch was a couple of hundred miles east in an area Stuart had hand-picked for its accessible water, abundant grasses, and sheltered areas. When the winter of 1886-1887 took two-thirds of their cattle, Stuart walked away from the business. Steadfast as ever, Kohrs nursed it back to health and eventually enjoyed even greater wealth.

The Grant-Kohrs Ranch exists today as a national historic site, preserved much as it was during the turn of the century and the early 1900s. Once 25,000 acres large, the land had been reduced to 1,000 acres in Kohrs' lifetime and is now 226 acres. The ranch buildings are situated alongside the Clark Fork of the Columbia River. Later, around 1907, railroad tracks were laid past the ranch, making it easy to ship cattle to market.

The main house, built in 1862, was described by the *Montana Post* as the finest in Montana. "It appears as if it had been lifted by the chimneys from the bank of the St. Lawrence, and dropped down in Deer Lodge Valley. It has twenty-eight windows, with green-painted shutters, and looks very pretty." The white, wood-frame two story house was long and rectangular. In 1890, Kohrs added a brick wing onto the back to provide room for his growing family. He had met and married Augusta Kruse on a trip to Cincinnati in 1868, and since that time she had brought warmth, style, and grace to the ranch house.

Not far from the main house was bunkhouse row. This was where the cowboys and ranch hands slept, ate, and spent their time in bad weather. Included in this group of buildings was the kitchen, where the bunkhouse cook whipped up plain but hearty fare to serve the hands. The ice house was built in the 1880s. Ice cut from winter ponds was stored under sawdust for use in the summer. With the advent of electric refrigeration, this building was converted to a tack room.

The long barn was used to stable horses. Alongside it was a small barn in which a single stallion was kept. Stallions were stabled separately to prevent fighting, and the ranch had several stallion barns. There were also barns for draft horses, oxen, and dairy cows.

Kohrs' partner in this ranch was his half-brother, John Bielenberg. Both died in the 1920s, and Kohrs' grandson, Conrad Kohrs Warren, took over the ranch. His work to preserve the ranch led to its being declared in 1972 a National Historic Site to provide "an understanding of the frontier cattle era of the nation's history."

The main street of a typical cattle town. This is Dodge City, Kansas.
(Photo courtesy of Kansas State Historical Society.)

DRIVING THE HERDS NORTH

By the 1860s, the fledgling cattle industry in Montana had finally taken hold, and Texas ranchers were starting to get back on their feet after the Civil War. The U.S. Army, no longer occupied with war, had turned to fighting Indians.

Nelson Story had first come to Montana in search of gold. He turned out to be one of the lucky ones—his findings at Alder Gulch were worth $30,000! Rather than squander this sizable pile of money, in 1886 he decided to buy cattle in Texas and drive them north to Montana. He could butcher some and sell the meat, as the Stuarts and Conrad Kohrs were doing. The others he would breed to start his own herd.

Story was a man of foresight and perseverance—he had to be. He was the first man to drive Texas cattle into Montana. It was a venture fraught with complications from beginning to end. First of all, when he got to Kansas, he found he was unwelcome—no Texas cattle were allowed to enter the state because of the Texas cattle fever scare. He had to take the Santa Fe Trail instead, circling around the perimeter of the state. In Wyoming he encountered another obstacle—this time in the form of attacking Indians. There was a skirmish, and the next day the Indians stampeded the cattle in hopes of kidnapping them. Story, not one to come this far and give up easily, went after the Indians and retrieved most of the cattle. Meanwhile, the commanding officer at nearby Fort Reno had decided that Story was stirring up the Indians needlessly and should not pass. Story ignored him and sneaked past the fort at night. He finally reached Montana in December—the end of a long, treacherous journey.

Other people had found closer markets for Texas cattle. In 1866, Charles Goodnight and Oliver Loving set out to drive 2,000 steers north from Texas. They were challenged by inhospitable Indians and even more inhospitable land.

Charles Goodnight established the Goodnight-Loving Trail with Oliver Loving.
(Photo courtesy of Colorado State Historical Society.)

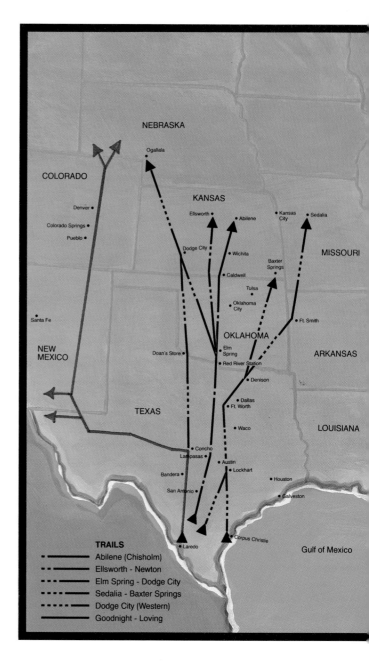

TRALS

- - - - Abilene (Chisholm)
- - - - Ellsworth - Newton
- - - - Elm Spring - Dodge City
- - - - Sedalia - Baxter Springs
- - - - Dodge City (Western)
——— Goodnight - Loving

Lack of water and patches of quicksand made their trip harrowing. When they reached Fort Sumner in New Mexico, they sold part of the herd to the army; the rest they drove into Colorado and sold to a Denver cattle trader, John Iliff. Their rough journey paid off handsomely, and they proved that their route, which came to be called the Goodnight-Loving Trail, was possible to travel.

Goodnight and Loving kept up a brisk trade between Texas and the territory to the north. The same Union Pacific tracks that ran past Abilene and Ellsworth were now entering Colorado, and Iliff had a contract to supply the railroad workers with beef. That meant a ready market for Goodnight and Loving's Texas cattle. Fortunes were not easily made and traveling was hazardous. During one trip, Loving was attacked by Indian raiders and was killed.

Goodnight soon turned to ranching instead of trail driving, setting up a ranch in Colorado. He lost the ranch in the Panic of 1873, when the banks failed and the price of beef plummeted. Goodnight resumed ranching a few years later, choosing the Texas panhandle as the place to start his Red River Ranch. He eventually prospered and became an important figure in Texas history.

In 1857, Iliff left Ohio for Kansas, raised some money, opened a store, and bought a 160 acre farm. Two years later, he sold the store and bought an ox-train of merchandise. This he took to Denver to sell to the miners. Soon he began trading in cattle, supplying nearby locations as well as shipping beef to Chicago. He bought Texas cattle for ten to fifteen dollars a head, fattened them up on his land for a year or so, and then sold them for up to three times as much. His expenses were few, and like other ranchers of the time, he actually owned little of the land on which his animals grazed. Iliff became a prominent rancher in Colorado and Wyoming with extensive land holdings in both states.

THE OPEN RANGE

*L*ike parts of Colorado, Wyoming had an abundance of good grazing land, and most of it was public domain. One often-repeated story tells of a man who was traveling on the Oregon Trail in 1864, bound for Utah. A sudden snowstorm on the Laramie Plains forced him to abandon his cart and turn his oxen loose while he went on to the nearest settlement for shelter. When he returned in the spring to see if he could salvage the cart or its contents, he expected to find his oxen dead. Instead, they were alive and healthy. All winter, they had been eating dry grass that had been preserved just under the snow.

This story and variations on it were passed around the West, and cattle drovers began to look at Wyoming in a new light. They realized that if they drove their cattle to Wyoming in the fall, the cattle would feed all winter long. Soon Wyoming was seen not merely as a thoroughfare, but as a destination.

Wyoming's good year-round grazing made it an attractive place to establish a ranch, and during the 1870s, many people did just that. Some were already cattle owners, and they came with their herds. Others bought herds there. Many ranches, especially those of absentee owners, were bought and sold on the basis of book tally, the number of cattle estimated to be in the herd. The cattle were not actually counted, and the number was changed to reflect sales, purchases, calves, and any other changes.

Many of Wyoming's early ranchers were foreign-born. John W. Myers, and Englishman, started his ranch in 1860. His was the first Wyoming brand to be recorded. Another Englishman, Richard Ashworth, founded the Z Bar T in 1882. In 1901, he sold it to Louis Phelps, who was artist Charles Russell's publisher. Phelps bought several more ranches in the same area, about fifty miles east of Yellowstone Park, consolidating them under the name of Pitchfork Ranch. The Pitchfork had been previously owned by Otto Frank, a German. Phelps' extended ranching operation remains in the family today and is run by his great-granddaughter and her husband.

Round-up, a busy day in ranch country.
(Photo courtesy of Wyoming State Archives.)

Above, Captain James Cook as a young man.

Below, he is shown with his friend Short Bull.

One of Nebraska's most prominent ranchers was James Cook. Like Charles Goodnight, he was a trail driver (among other things) before he became a rancher. Cook was descended from the famous English navigator and explorer, Captain James Cook. Raised in Michigan, he left home for Leavenworth, Kansas, when he was fifteen. There he got a job herding Texas cattle, and later worked on a Texas ranch. After five trips north on drives for the ranch, he finally decided to stay in Wyoming.

Cook and another man teamed up to hunt and supply deer and antelope meat for the town of Cheyenne and the Union Pacific Railroad. They also conducted hunting parties for groups from the East and from Europe. Cook did so well that he managed to amass $10,000, an extremely large sum at that time. In 1882, he and an Englishman started the WS Ranch in New Mexico, but Cook soon sold out and returned to Cheyenne to buy his father-in-law's ranch, the O4, in northwestern Nebraska, about one hundred and fifty miles from Cheyenne.

Cook's life intersected with several historic moments in western history. He was in New Mexico during Geronimo's last attempt to flee and met the lieutenant who was sent to capture him; he was in Pine Ridge when the Massacre at Wounded Knee Creek (close to Pine Ridge) occurred. Pine Ridge, the home of Chief Red Cloud, a Sioux, was just across the South Dakota border from the O4. Cook and Red Cloud had often visited and had considerable respect for each another. Cook was the one to discover fossils on the grounds of the O4 Ranch. This area, now preserved as the Agate Fossil Beds National Monument, brought many famous scientists to the O4. Cook's son, Harold, inspired by his early exposure to the field, became a distinguished paleontologist.

In *Longhorn Cowboy*, one of several books by James Cook, he reflects on the life of the cowboy, whether ranch owner or ranch hand: "That life near to nature, lacking in excesses and frills, tended to make men. Most of the boys I knew were honest, generous to a fault, respectful to women and to the aged. The sunshine and wind and hard riding of the plains helped, I believe, to develop self-reliant and efficient men. I look with pride back to those old cowboys."

Above, the den in Captain Cook's ranch house in Agate, Nebraska.

Below, the ranch house was built by Captain Cook in 1892. The coach was used by the proud owner to show guests around. Tom Powell, the driver, was a driver of the Yellowstone Stage. In the coach are the Captain, Harold, and Margaret Cook. (All photos courtesy of Nebraska State Historical Society.)

The Cheyenne Club, Cheyenne, Wyoming, 1888. (Photo courtesy of Wyoming State Archives.)

STOCKMENS' ASSOCIATIONS

As cattle ranchers encountered more and more difficulties, they found strength in numbers. Small groups began to organize into stock growers' associations. The Wyoming Stock Growers' Association started out in 1873 as the Laramie County Stock Growers' Association, founded by ten ranchers. It soon developed into a major organization with over four hundred members representing business in six states.

The Association set up rules to fight cattle rustling, and those caught altering brands on cattle were severely punished. As a source of income, the Association claimed all mavericks, unbranded motherless calves, and branded them with an M. When sold at auction, the money went into the Association's coffers to be used for operating expenses.

Stock growers' associations soon became powerful organizations; belonging to one had social, political, and economic benefits for a cattleman. Soon they became a way of controlling who ranched in a particular area. Any stock grower could apply for membership, but not everyone was admitted. In some parts of the country, big ranchers simply didn't want any more herds grazing in the area. Without the backing of the organization, smaller ranchers often got squeezed out. Some moved, trying to find less populated areas.

In 1884, the first national convention of cattlemen took place in St. Louis. At this momentous event, over 1,300 cattlemen gathered to combine their forces. They controlled a significant amount of money and land, and they had serious concerns to convey to Washington. By the time they were finished, the National Cattle and Horse Growers' Association of the United States was formed. One of its first acts was to ask for governmental help in three areas:

to stop the Indians from stealing their cattle and horses, to establish a National Cattle Trail north from Texas, and to lease government-owned grazing land on a long term basis.

According to one 1885 newspaper account, "every city of any note" had one or more social clubs, which "exerted a wide and beneficial influence." The Cheyenne Club, in Cheyenne, Wyoming, was founded in 1880 by twelve young cattlemen from wealthy Eastern families. For them, ranching was more a pastime than a livelihood. As one historian of this period put it, "they furnished examples of how one could spend money on something more than cows and land."

To make the club exclusive, membership was

limited to fifty (it was later raised to two hundred). The club had rooms for those who wanted to spend the night in town, a fine dining room, a library filled with books and subscriptions to national newspapers and magazines, and a billiards room. Unruly behavior was not tolerated, and membership could be suspended or terminated for violating the rules. Just as today, these social clubs were the scene for much business conversation as well as for pleasure.

A Wyoming historian has noted that "the club was not merely a meeting place of cattlemen. Unofficially, many of the Wyoming laws were born there, as legislators chatted over their food and drink." The club served as a base of operations for cattlemen who were not from Wyoming and was often home to absentee cattle owners from many different countries. Because of that, the Cheyenne Club gained world-wide fame.

Many a business deal was made over drinks at the Cheyenne Club.

THE ROUGH RIDER

*T*eddy Roosevelt was 25 when he first came to the Dakota Badlands on a hunting trip. Taking the train west, he got off at Medora, a cattle town in present-day North Dakota. Roosevelt was born and raised in New York City and held a degree from Harvard. He had inherited a tidy sum of money from his father, enough to live off the income, and his political career had already begun. The year before, he had been elected a state legislator. Doctors had told him, however, that he had bad lungs and hadn't much time to live.

Those who saw him on his arrival out West would certainly have believed the doctors' diagnosis. He was skinny, pale, and fragile-looking, with thick, round glasses. He was immediately nicknamed "Four Eyes." They took one look at this puny specimen and wondered how he would be able to survive on a hunting expedition. He,

on the other hand, saw this expedition as an opportunity to strengthen himself through physical exercise and exposure to fresh, clean air.

From the beginning, Roosevelt exhibited a surprising resilience. He hired a hunting guide, Joe Ferris, and despite five straight days of rain, they went out looking for buffalo. When at last they found some, a charging bull caused Roosevelt's horse to rear and Roosevelt was hit with his own gun. Even that didn't deter his enthusiasm.

During this trip, Ferris took him to the Chimney Butte Ranch (also called the Maltese Cross after its brand), just outside Medora. This ranch was managed by Ferris' brother and another man for absentee owners. By the end of his two-week stay, Roosevelt had become so taken with ranch life that he decided to buy out the owners of the Chimney Butte!

Roosevelt's ranching career spanned only a few years, but it changed him immeasurably. He soon developed into a competent horseman and cattleman, and he gained great respect for ranchers. "There are very few businesses so absolutely legitimate as stock-raising and so beneficial to the nation at large," he wrote in *Ranch Life and the Hunting Trail*, published in 1888. "A successful stock-grower must not only be shrewd, thrifty, patient, and enterprising, but he must also possess qualities of personal bravery, hardihood, and self-reliance to a degree not demanded in the least by any mercantile occupation in a community long settled. Stock-

Medora, North Dakota, from 1883-1906. (All photos courtesy of North Dakota State Historical Society.)

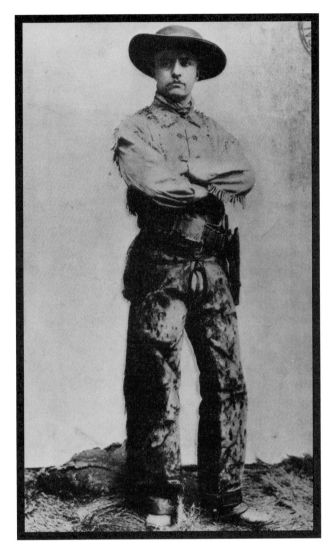

Young Teddy Roosevelt came to North Dakota as a tenderfoot from the east.

men are in the West the pioneers of civilization, and their daring and adventurousness make the after settlement of the region possible. The whole country owes them a great debt."

The year after he bought the Chimney Rock, Roosevelt's wife died from a childbirth-related illness. The loss caused him to spend even more time on his ranch, and he bought a second ranch about thirty miles north of the first. Today, much of the area between Medora and this ranch, which Roosevelt named the Elkhorn, is preserved as the Theodore Roosevelt National Park.

Roosevelt wrote many books and articles about his experiences in the West; some served to correct Eastern misconceptions of the place. He noted, for instance, that cowboys are "very good fellows, and the most determined and effective foes of real law breakers, such as horse and cattle thieves, murderers, etc. Few of the

outrages quoted in Eastern papers as their handiwork are such in reality."

Roosevelt withdrew from the ranching business after the winter of 1886-1887, when much of his herd was wiped out. He had remarried in 1886, and his political career was on the upswing. In 1898, the U.S. declared war against Spain. As a lieutenant colonel, Roosevelt organized the First U.S. Volunteer Cavalry. Their nickname, the Rough Riders, reflected their leader's "Wild West" past, and the unit was immortalized by their charge up Kettle Hill at San Juan. Two years later, he was elected William McKinley's Vice President. The following year McKinley was assassinated and he was thrust into the Presidency.

Roosevelt began ranching when the industry was young, and when North Dakota was still a territory and not a state. In his experiences were combined two very different aspects of the same country: the educated, wealthy Easterner, and the adventurous, hard-working, self-made Westerner.

The presidential years.

BARBED WIRE

*I*t is doubtful that Joseph Glidden knew how he would influence the history of the West when he invented barbed wire. He had been fascinated by his neighbor's invention, a wooden fence with sharp spikes sticking out of the top rail. He took this idea and translated it into a string of wire, with barbs sticking out at odd angles. Strung between wooden poles, this wire fencing was considerably cheaper than an all wood fence. The barbs served to convince animals to stay on their own side of the fence—a plain wire fence was just no match for a stampeding herd of cattle. In 1874, Glidden was given patent number 157,124 for his invention.

Glidden began manufacturing the wire, but

it was John Gates, a young salesman, who saw its potential for cattlemen. He took it to San Antonio and staged a dramatic demonstration. He built a corral of barbed wire in the town square and had twenty-five longhorns driven excitedly into the corral. They charged at the fence, but it held, and so they backed off and tried it again. After this scene was repeated several times, they finally gave up. The crowd was impressed. Gates started taking orders for the wire.

At first many ranchers resisted the wire, preferring to think of the range as free. Some even sent out cowboys to cut the fences others had erected. In the end, though, barbed wire enabled the powerful cattle kings to fence off acres and acres of land cheaply—land that was actually in the public domain. In Texas, so much barbed wire was strung up that one county seat was cut off from the rest of the state! Even mail carriers complained that their routes were blocked by these wire fences.

Sometimes cattlemen failed to think things through before putting up the wire. Barbed wire fences played a sad part in the winter disaster of 1886-1887. Many cattle, whose instinct before a storm is to find shelter, found their way to safety blocked by the fences. They were caught out on the open range and suffered a torturous death.

RANGE WARS

*B*esides fighting the weather, the cattle rustler, and the occasional Indian, the rancher was beginning to face a new enemy: the homesteader. The Homestead Act of 1862 gave 160 acres of free land to anyone who agreed to settle on it. By the 1880s, much of this government land had been fenced in by cattlemen.

The homesteader who ignored the fences and settled in on the land anyway did so at considerable risk. Very likely he would be visited by a contingent of cowboys and told to leave. If he didn't he might be shot. Homesteaders' complaints finally got back to Washington and, in 1885, Congress passed a law that prohibited fencing in public domain land. Ranchers complied by having their hired hands lay claim to all the sections within their fenced area. Some homesteaders fought back by killing cattle that entered their land.

Some farmers who refused to leave were burned out.

The Johnson County Cattle Raiders, 1892.
(Photo courtesy of Wyoming State Archives.)

In Wyoming, this feud culminated in the Johnson County War of 1892. Johnson County was in northern Wyoming, and the homesteaders there had formed their own association. They rounded up "stray" cattle and marked them with their own brands. This enraged the cattle owners. A group of men, not sanctioned by the Wyoming Stock Growers' Association, secretly formed a plan to eliminate these rustlers. They hired professional gunmen and cut the telegraph wires that ran out of Buffalo, the closest town. The gunmen killed the homesteaders on the KC Ranch and set fire to their buildings. Then they progressed to the next homesteader's ranch. The sheriff in Buffalo organized a group of men to fight back, but because of the cut telegraph lines, he could not wire for extra help. When news of the war between the cattlemen and the homesteaders eventually did reach Washington, the President sent troops from the closest fort.

The men who were arrested were taken to Cheyenne to stand trial, but no one was willing to be a witness against them. Finally they were released, with neither side winning the war. The cattlemen weren't punished, nor had they suc-

ceeded in stopping the homesteaders' rustling.

As the amount of free land dwindled, cattlemen also found themselves in competition with sheep ranchers. The cattlemen claimed that sheep ruined the land for cattle because they would not graze on land where sheep had been. At first the cattlemen tried stampeding steers through the flocks of sheep, killing some and scattering others. Sometimes they drove them off cliffs or lay down poison to kill them. On occasion, their tactics turned even more violent. Some sheepherders found themselves face to face with men with gunny sacks covering their heads. The gunmen would kill the sheep and the sheepherder and set fire to the wagon.

By this time, sheepherders had established a Wyoming Wool Growers' Association. After one particularly grisly attack, the organization offered a reward for information leading to the arrest of the murderers. This time, five men were convicted, and law and order was restored. In time, the cattlemen grew to accept their new neighbors on the range, and some eventually started running sheep in addition to cattle. As it turned out, the same land could be used for both cattle and sheep as long as cattle had the first turn. Sheep could graze on land that had already been used by cattle. Harmony, at least, prevailed.

CATTLE BRANDS

The cattle brand is the rancher's traditional mark of ownership. Brands are burned directly onto an animal's hide with a branding iron and remain there for life. There are several ways in which owners can mark their cattle, and they often decide on using a combination. Forms of identification can include the brand plus an earmark, wattle, or dewlap.

The earmark is a particular cut in a cow's ear. This cut can take many shapes—for example, a notch, a slice, or a hole punch—and it can be positioned anywhere along the right or left ear. The many options allow for a wide variety of combinations, all different.

Wattles are hanging flaps of skin made by cutting the skin and letting it heal. They can be positioned anywhere—on the shoulder, hip, tail, head or elsewhere. Dewlaps are slits in the skin in areas where the skin is already hanging or folded. These are usually found in the areas around the chin, jaw, and throat.

The hide brand did not originate in the Old West. Over four thousand years ago, Egyptians branded their animals to show ownership of herds. Throughout the centuries, owners of livestock have done the same. Branding was a standard procedure among the Spanish who introduced cattle to North America. The brand of Cortes, the conqueror of Mexico, consisted of three Latin crosses.

In North America, brands have been registered

since the 1600s, when English settlers recorded ownership of their herds. In the West, Richard H. Chisholm of Gonzales County, Texas, was the first to record his brand in 1832. It consisted of the initials H.C. underscored by a straight line.

In addition to owners' brands, cattle that were going to be driven on cattle trails were often given road brands. This brand signified that a cow in question was part of the trail herd and, more importantly, that unbranded cattle were not part of the herd. Another kind of brand was the county brand, a separate, additional brand on the neck that identified the animal as recorded in a certain county. This practice made it difficult for cattle rustlers to register stolen cattle.

During the last half of the 1800s, registration laws varied from place to place. In some states or territories, brands were registered with the county clerk, and in others they were registered at the state level or with the state livestock growers' association. Where county registration was the only requirement, the same brands were often duplicated in neighboring counties. This created confusion, since there was always a chance that cattle from two different herds carrying the same brand might wander, becoming intermingled. Today, most U.S. states and Canadian provinces have brand recording offices, and stock growers' associations also issue brand books that list the brands and their owners.

Brands are made up of a combination of letters, symbols, or numbers. They're designed to be read from top to bottom, outside to inside, or left to right. Chisholm's brand, described above, would read "H C Bar." A straight line is read as "bar." A straight line through a letter or symbol is known as a "cross," and at an angle, it's a "slash." A letter on its side is "lazy," with curves at its ends it is "running." Brands that are framed are known as "boxed brands." Unboxed brands are "open."

Reading brands correctly is an essential skill for cowhands and is known as "calling the brands." During the spring branding season, calves that had been born in the past year were cut out from the herd for branding and any other attention they might need. As he was bringing in the calf, the roper, known as the ketch hand, called out the brand of the mother. While the flankers were pinning the calf, the iron tender selected the proper brand and handed it to the brander. At the same time, the cutter made the earmark, dewlap, or wattle, while someone else administered immunization shots against disease.

If an animal was sold to another owner, the original owner added a "vent brand"—his brand with a line drawn through it signifying the transaction. The term comes from the Spanish word *venta,* which means sale. Then the new owner was free to add his brand. Cattle that changed hands many times became covered with brands, or, as the cowboys said, were "burnt till they looked like a brand book."

Sheepherders and farmers fenced in the range and changed the character of the West.
(Photo courtesy of Wyoming State Archives.)

IN THE DAYS OF THE CATTLE RANCHERS

1845	Texas becomes a state.
1846-1848	United States and Mexico enter into war over disputed land claims, resolved by a treaty ceding New Mexico, Texas, California, Arizona, Nevada, Utah, and part of Colorado to U.S.
1852	Richard King starts the Santa Gertrudis Ranch.
1857	Granville and James Stuart arrive in Montana.
1859	John W. Iliff arrives in Denver.
1861	Kansas becomes a state.
1861-1865	The Civil War divides the country.
1862	Congress passes the Homestead Act.
1862	Conrad Kohrs arrives in Montana.
1864	Laws are enacted to regulate marks and brands.
1866	Nelson Story drives the first herd of Texas cattle into Montana.
1866	Union Pacific Railroad reaches Abilene.
1866	Goodnight-Loving Trail established.
1867	Nebraska becomes a state.
1867	Union Pacific Railroad reaches Cheyenne.
1867	Joseph McCoy builds stockyards at Abilene.
1873	Bank panic sets off five-year depression and causes beef prices to fall.
1874	Glidden receives patent for barbed wire.
1876	Colorado becomes a state.
1880	The Cheyenne Club is formed.
1884	National Cattle and Horse Growers' Association is formed.
1884	Roosevelt buys first ranch in Dakota Territory.
1886-1887	Severe winter storm kills thousands of cattle and puts many small ranchers out of business.
1889	North Dakota, South Dakota, and Montana become states.
1890	Wyoming becomes a state.
1892	Johnson County War erupts between Wyoming cattlemen and homesteaders.